This
Much
I Can
Tell
You

This
Much
I Can
Tell
You

poems
David Rigsbee

Black
Lawrence
Press

Black
Lawrence
Press

www.blacklawrence.com

Executive Editor: Diane Goettel
Book and Cover Design: Amy Freels
Cover Art: "Fall Flickers," acrylic on unprimed canvas by Catherine Carr Whittemore

Copyright © 2017 David Rigsbee
ISBN: 978-1-62557-967-6

Published 2017 by Black Lawrence Press.
Printed in the United States.

For Liz

Contents

January

for Linda Gregg

Being a man, I was the least
among the shades
because of what I still carried.
I asked the caryatid to extend
her hand, but it was broken,
which is the way with stone.
There were several at the entrance,
but they were ornamental,
no longer load-bearing.
The dead would not have it.
The sun was sinking toward the rim,
I remember. I remember too
the poet said, it is more important
to walk across a field now
than to revisit the sorrows.

Oriole

Let me begin by telling you
how the oriole lit for a moment on the power line
as I sat, in thought, on my balcony perch
and fed myself with books, sentence after sentence,
above the ground squirrels, above the dogwood's reply
to the fleur-de-lis, above the hop and blink
that goes by unseen under the leaves.
I read word by word, syllable by syllable,
letters like wooden Hessians on a calliope lost at sea,
on their voyage from the Old World,
expressionless and yet expressive,
sinking in their stiff uniforms, bottle-straight, simple.
When I looked up, it was gone, the wire
still rocking as if it had made a musical note
on behalf of its player, a common bird
who made his own song in another forest.

A Certain Person

It was Auden, I believe, who said that
in a certain person's presence he felt
"incapable of doing anything base
or unloving." Walking past the flat
on St. Mark's Place, past the memorial
plaque that, until this year, bore his name,
I look ahead to the park where
the homeless line up, as black squirrels
hop down from the leafless trees
to forage in the dry grass, the same
grass where a tiny mouse, rescued
from someone's sink and carried
in a clear, half-pint container, now roams,
if mice can be said to roam.
And persons capable of doing both base
and unloving things stroll across the bricks
the way they do in pictures of promenades
of foreign capitals between the wars.
The homeless line holds steady
all afternoon, and from a loudspeaker
somewhere comes the clarinet I take
to be Artie Shaw's. From somewhere else
Lil Wayne answers. Neither could be
described as without difficulty. Shaw,
for instance, was married eight times.

Where is the Auden plaque now?
It must be someplace, even if
it's noplace. And when Shaw recorded
"Green Eyes," was there a mouse
in a sink somewhere wondering with his
tiny wit about the flatness and the whiteness
and the dark hole at the center?

The Silent "E"

I was looking at a picture. The Cure
was playing in the background. It was one
of those gravel roads that begins wide
in the foreground—barbed fences in need
of fixing on either side, cincture-like, all
following a curve—until, only a small way
up from the frame, topping a little hill, it
quickly shrank from view, its vanishing point
a ditch of prairie grass. More hills followed,
rising where the road ended, though to say
that they rose doesn't alter the fact
that if you squinted for just a moment,
it was neither hill rising, nor hill sloping,
but horizons superseding each other.
A band of steel-colored mountains, mid-frame,
appeared like a stratum from deep time,
showing how some species likely succumbed.
Above this, Constable clouds froze in place.
The rest, the upper third, was wholly sky.
To insert yourself in such a landscape
is to feel like the silent "e" in Anne, to be
there, and yet not at the same time.
For something happened that the photo
can only register as the yearning one brings
to something gone, the full empty landscape

so without you. It is as if you are part
of its perfection. You could remain
for hours, a pilgrim before the last shrine,
which was also the first, and though
it was finally put by, a picture, lost,
who would deny it was yours alone?

Max and the Promise

*"I had a dream of purity
and I have lived in the desert ever since."*
—George Garrett

One day, Max Steele called me into his office
ostensibly to discuss short fiction,
but the news of Mishima's *seppuku*
had swept through the department
earlier that morning. I was a student
and as sensitive to literary rumors
and gossip as any bumblebee
riding the first spring breeze. Outside,
the SDS taunted the Young Republicans,
while frat boys in their Madras shorts
talked trash to passing hippies.
But in far-off Japan, after charging Mt. Fuji
in Nutcracker uniforms, the Shield Society
had drawn attention to the tiger's paw.
It was not enough to be a writer,
even reaching the Nobel stratosphere.
Only death would seal the deal,
only death reverse the dishonor,
heal the emasculation. So he prepared
in his Victorian house for years:
real death after role-playing,

ceremonial oblivion after deep hurt.
His last words before disembowelment
and beheading: "I don't think
they heard me very well." Max swung
around in his chair and said, "promise me
you'll never kill yourself!" Startled as I was,
I did. I saw Max in Nixon a few years later,
when we learned how the President
had led Kissinger to the carpet and prayers
in the Oval Office. I forgave Nixon
when I realized he was human, and I made
the gentle Max loosen his grip
when I saw how he, unlike his name,
fit so snugly in his little patch
of ground, a plaque commemorating
what forgetfulness routinely undoes.
Even Jesus would have failed
Max's oath: it's no wonder
such promises hold but for five minutes,
no wonder self-destruction mirrors
self-creation: how could it not?
Max lay long wasting before he died.
My niece torched herself in a motel room
at 18, prepared and afraid, having made
no promise to a teacher, embracing
self-immolation as the cure for love.
And then there was my brother.
I have seen the end of my rope
lying in a coil, and you couldn't tell

if it was a snake or a garden hose
or just a length of rope. Max and Mishima
are dust; the niece I never knew:
a picture. My brother, the silence
before and after the poem. All these
chapters feeding the effrontery and sorrow.
Empson admired a Buddha head
which was chiseled with a hooded cobra
risen in glory inches away and trained
to protect his double face.

Oversize Load

Of course, they left the "d" off.
People don't see the use
of the past participle anymore.
Perhaps they don't understand it,
its simple descriptive power.
Perhaps they have no feel for suffixes,
as for a thing grown irrelevant over time.
After all, docking the past
can be a good idea, sometimes.
I was fleeing depression that day
and headed out to the interstate.
I will not bore you with details.
There I listened to Roy Orbison
assault eternity with his high notes,
followed by the "55 Essential Tracks"
of The Everly Brothers. It was a lot
of emotion to cover, and the highway
seemed as good a place as any, since
the feeling of flight did its faultless
parody of transport and blended
with the changing landscape,
the humble farms transmogrifying
into the tacky suburbs that replaced them.
Before I knew it, I was over the state line
into Virginia, which I am reminded

is "for lovers," as the billboard
used to say (*only* for lovers, you
had to wonder?). The smaller truck,
the one with the bad grammar,
used flashing lights to keep creepers
at a distance. No worries: no one
was eager to pass, anyway.
What I couldn't yet process was
that there was another up ahead:
two pairs of trucks, each
with a smaller, trailing pickup
with revolving lights and that sign,
and before it, a squat semi, where
chained to each flatbed like Prometheus
after he had irked Zeus
was a *tank*—an Abrams tank.
Twice I did a double-take
because what I could finally make out,
when I was pulling up closer,
was the barrel of the cannon, lowered
and trained squarely at me as I came on.
To what battles these were being sent
or returning—as is more likely—from,
there was no hint, only brown dirt
dried in the sprockets and tracks.
I thought: this is what poetry is,
although where my thought was leading
I wasn't exactly sure. At least it was
a thought, not some random memory

hung with the taffy of association
or an image dredged up from an image bank,
the private person's private store.
But the fact is, you grieve, and you
stare down the barrel of a cannon
at the same time, and you don't know why
there should be a connection,
or how you got in range of such a thing.
And then it happens again, as if
to say, *sic semper* to chance.
Yet something yokes them both
in the mind and, as Wallace Stevens
would have said, the mind of the poem.
I have often noticed it, and I know
that you must have too. Let the poem
teach, let it point a finger and declaim
as the highway unrolls seemingly forever,
in the face of grief and the barrel's mouth.
There was nowhere you could have arrived.
And the dark heart just sit there.

Ferguson

Protesters down Canal. Ferguson
in flames. Chanting. I had taken
the train from 59th St., after
a dinner party with foundation
trustees, monied people of the left
and a playwright who wrote
the double plight of assimilated
Muslims, of which he was one.
He spoke of what he had learned
from Roth, Bellow, and Potok
on the way to the Pulitzer.
London staged him. Chicago,
Lincoln Center, and Broadway.
I walked down the sidewalk next
to the heavy stone entrances,
the liveried doormen. I was
thinking again of my beloved
who never accepted my suit
or acquitted the fabric of its tear.
My daughter leapt up and flew
down the steps in pajamas
to join the crowd. I thought
of Bogan's lines: "I shall not see
the face of my friend" and
"the country whereto I go."

This Much I Can Tell You

Sometimes it feels as if the mind
will seal itself up and you can go
a great distance without ever seeing
those who ever spoke your name.
You hear everything from cacophony
to a symphony played on instruments,
provenance unknown, stored out of sight
long ago. It is a closed system
but vast, and time unfolds there too,
unrelenting, nothing in abeyance,
like animal eyes suddenly appearing
in the roadside weeds and fields,
through which the highway plunges,
and on it a car traveling, not speeding,
not hanging back either. This much
I can tell you: there is smoke
beyond the mind, to which the mind turns,
as to a burning house, flames raging,
spurting from the second story windows.
Shouldn't you be running up the lawn?
Shouldn't there be, in truth, more fires?

'68

I was reminded of the Wallace rally
back in '68, the country music molding
the crowd, the police cordon complete
with wooden billy clubs, my friends and I
in the rear, sarcastic and quiet, dissolving
our contempt in the dish of humor.
I've waited nearly 50 years to write this,
how we did nothing else, but hung back,
his "pointy-headed intellectuals," that
sunny day. It was like walking up
to the glass at an aquarium to see funny-
looking fish pausing and staring back,
each species regarding the other.
Wallace was right about us: when the police
shoved back we scattered. But the little man
didn't miss a beat, arms flailing, sometimes
windmilling, fanning the rhetoric. Our skulls
escaped, but fear never outweighed our
satisfaction. We repaired to a bar, smoked
Larks and drank loudly, as college students do,
pulling off impressions and quips. Where
are my comrades now? I don't even remember
who they were. I suppose it's time for apostrophes,
for some invocations to the forces beyond,
but that seems maudlin now, even pretentious.

I do remember my last glimpse of the man
as I was running. I could still see that
leering mouth that worked the crowd
into frightening self-righteousness: everything
had been stolen from them, and the time
had come to take it back. They didn't
even notice the commotion in the rear:
some kids in need of correction.
There were fairground pennants too, rippling
onstage, the kind you see now at used-car lots.
I have traded in my memories for images.
But he was right: everything is stolen.
The highway tires do their work, pressing
down hard, until the road kill becomes a slick,
and predictably, without notice, the road again.
The ignorant have a right to be personally offended.
Even a racist country boy could see that.

Clothespins

In the end, Hegel says, it's all war.
But we're not at the end, are we?
We are somewhere along the spectrum
marking what was, like the way
my mother used to leave the clothespins
on the line at the very place she had
placed wet sheets, pants, towels, socks.
They were stories too, the clothespins,
though what they marked, in light
of early death and despair is hard to say.
And was there one for regret?
There should have been many for that
and the line long. I had thought if only
momentarily about Hegel because
I was also thinking about the power
of language to bring about love
in the face of the failure of language
to revive that same love. An old
professor, now deceased, once told me
that he had dreamt the last words
of Shakespeare, viz., "words are fleas."
He was a professor of drama,
of course. What other person
would have such a dream, both
demented and true? For if words

are true, Hegel is right, and the poem
that drew the lover in gave way
to the useless one that couldn't sing
her into staying. And yet, the fleas
get attention too, no doubt about that.
I will never forget a September Saturday
I went to a football game at LSU.
At halftime, the announcer barked
that former Governor Jimmie Davis
would lead us all in a song.
A tiny geriatric in a cowboy hat
mounted the endzone stage and stood
with his guitar before a mic
He strummed and sang the first words.
Suddenly a hundred thousand fans
in that great bowl rose as if on cue
and began singing, "You are
my sunshine, my only sunshine..."
Everyone had the words, as they say,
by heart, and I too fell under the sway
of the mass enchantment, finding
myself having to deal with hot tears,
yet singing along in a choir of a hundred
thousand souls with the one-term,
one-hit governor from Lost Time
who had such sweetness, such sorrow—
a Republican no less. As I say,
such sorrow, such collective sorrow,
marked in a song in the heart of everybody.

Armature

The building was immense and empty.
I hoped Bede was right and that sparrow
would find the skylight and fly
his crazy route from one emptiness
to another, like the swallows in Wal-Mart
that flicker and dart among the girders.

When Zeus showed up, I pointed out
this was my soul, abandoned
and cheapened by consolation.

But I found I was addressing the air,
arm extended in frozen emphasis
like the statue of Saddam Hussein
the elated mob toppled and jumped on
revealing its cheap, spinal armature,
before peace and the real war began.

Next the Sky

Think bigger, you said, *think*
how it looks from roof level, think
next the sky. And so I did.
I followed the shrinking figure
as it seemed to float down the street
and finally turn into a period, waiting,
it seemed, to make a telling conclusion,
the last bar of an old drinking song,
when the men fall silent and look
at their hands, having no further use
for their amazing instruments.

The Takeaway

It was as if a small reckoning
had taken place because I
looked down and all I could see
was my napkin fallen like a sail
over the pontoons of my shoes,
pointing in your direction.
And when I raised my eyes
there were our plates and scraps,
a residual rim of sauce on one
like a distant coastline;
the other in similar disarray:
bones, tomato wheels lying by.
I averted my gaze, because I knew
yours was there, patient, waiting,
with that steadfast charity.
And that was the takeaway,
so I walked down the street
skirting the river, wind still warm
from the finished summer,
clouds starting to assemble.
Someone passed and I heard,
"I am of the opinion that…"
I crossed the street and stepped
down the subway stairs
like an Academy Award Winner

who knows to pause after such steps
before moving on to the transport
in the very place where the actual
stops, and the symbolic begins.

Some Only Stick

I do often think about it,
as surely as the beard of Lytton Strachey
pointed to the center of the earth.
The question arose,
was silence a kind of literary criticism?
As usual, I came down squarely
on both sides, led first by passion
and my headlong devotions,
and then by the comforting thought
of the noiseless hole in the world.
Oh, the succor of that thing.
I read Valéry, and went about
like a scientist conducting his experiment,
in this case in a graveyard
where inappropriate music lilted
through the leaves: Sing it!
it seemed to say. The pain
will stay like the bones and not rise.
To which the bones neither assented
nor protested. It was as if
they somehow knew all along
another breeze would follow
and yet another. And some
would have music, and others
certainly not; some with fiddle and some

only stick with which to mark a beat;
higher above, geese and order,
and higher still just this idea
that haunted about the emptiness, a wisp
you see crossing the moon, or miss,
as the case may be, if you are
watching, instead, the road.

Falsetto

I saw Frankie Avalon and Lou Christie once
with their shirts off. It was outside, May,
Louisiana, their modest torsos QT-ed, each
wearing a Rolex the sun would catch and raise
to a dazzle, as they lifted the mic up delicately
to their Elvis-imitating mouths and belted
the fistful of fervid hits for which they
had formed the oldies revue aimed at ironists
and romantic questers like me. Why we
rose to stand there, the sweating congregation
of us, I can't say, except we were served
by mock enthusiasm, the *en-theo*, or God-in-us
we came away feeling. And not Avalon,
with his Hebe-like face and curled locks,
whose routine tenor rode a wave of melody
until it petered out like foam. It was Christie,
with that screechy larynx, as if fleeing fire,
who seemed suddenly yanked from earth.
He had discovered he had two faces,
and the shock of realization propelled him
upward, hair frozen, trunk sleek, defenseless
and bony. Yet he was suddenly striving toward God
because only He could rescue the Everyman
otherwise ensnared in banalities of the mortal coil,
not the least of which was failure at love

and the subsequent covering up to restore
a semblance of equilibrium. But everyone knew
it was merely, in Salinger's phrase, sad-making.
It was not worth the saccharine, much less
a voice taking wing in an unnatural register
to knock at the door of such a vapid mystery
as failure. It was as if the emotion's allegorical
figure stood before self-esteem long enough
to allow forgetting to melt it all away.
This is my theme: how a pop star poked
a hole in the sky and flew into it so that
heaven would know what we have always known:
that one face was not enough to be true.
When I understood that, I could have
laid my treasures at his feet, declared him
my King, except that he, Lou Christie,
was of course a knockoff and moreover headed
to the bin where records go, where they become
trash never to be recycled beyond a paltry
decade or two, so as to be closer to us,
as we are music to death itself, a ratio
pleasing no doubt to the Heaven of Plato,
endlessly soaring, high-pitched, and perfect.

Ten-Second Delay

That Blake etching, the angel hovering
over a skeleton, holding a trumpet.
We were unable to hear its note,
or watch the skeleton stir, at first daintily,
then the winching pull, accompanied
by sighs and the clicking of bones as it
sits upright. Nor could we see.
It's a surmise, which brings
me to her mouth, now talking
as our eyes locked across a small
chasm, her face against itself,
sprinkling confectioner's sugar atop
an ordinary, unassuming bread.
The food of love for the fools of love.
It's said TV cameras enforced
a ten-second delay so that
if Wallenda fell, the cameras could
cut away, and have nothing revealed,
although a body plunging through
space travels like the note
from the angel's instrument.
Therefore the Africans on Canal St.
pursue us with phrases, "Rolex! Rolex!
Vuitton! Vuitton!" the obviously fake
and shoddy goods pressed upon us

on every side in the voices of angels
in Blake, in the gauntlet of Blake.
The car horns mount up into a brass
section. The policeman, a conductor,
lets some through. Others must sing
if honking is song, their squalid
heartbreaking anthem, that fits my love
for the lost cause it must have been.
For each was armed with a tenderness
like an arctic creature melting into the wild,
truly long gone for the other, and from
the other, when dinner led us out
into the night, the ceaseless traffic,
where we parted, so filled and filling
with unspeakable acceptance
we hesitated, before the pattern
of divergence gave way to wind
and cold, first things without agenda,
which was loneliness as we felt it.

Empire Service

It seems to take longer than usual
for the train to emerge from the tunnel.
Broken buildings, then rocky banks
of the river and weedy masses rushing
past. At Tarrytown, the phone glows,
but it's not a real light, not a light
you can read by. Rather, it's your face.

I have lost the power to explain myself.

At Croton, a wedge of ducks
makes way across the still inlet.
Farther out, swans. Two of them.
Just for a second do they register.
Weeds are everywhere out there.
And yet it's winter and they're dead too,
though still standing at attention,
still presenting themselves somehow
to the vines, the trunks, the sky.
Then off in the distance I hear the horns,
warning of the train, and I'm on it.

Unfriend Me

I used to crank up that Toni Braxton song
when I drove through the mountains of Virginia
at night on my way to a certain apartment
on a hill. And I used to find my edge
at the tip of my finger, some unbefitting
thing, some toy Rubicon, and press Enter.
I was one inch above the law, above
public order and good behavior, but,
I could argue, within the standard deviation.
Meantime, I was this other person too. Now
the part you have to believe, since unbelief
has been my downfall, is that I put the truth
out there unvarnished, yet weirdly shining,
like some creature just discovered next
to a volcano vent at the bottom of the ocean.
I put it out there to be examined, named,
prized maybe, then put appropriately away.
The way we do. The way scientists do
because at some point they have to get
home. So much is going on in the ordinary
there's no need to track the specimens.
There are containers and labels at the ready
for that. As for home, the man finds love
in the trivial urgencies, the flotsam and small
change, homework, bills, dishes, whatever,

and later that night the husband drapes
his arm over his wife and covers her crotch
with his big, plain hand before the first dream
is even finished, and she, also dreaming,
covers his hand and tenderly pulls it away.

Composition

And then there was the Greek poet
who heard a man had died upstairs
in the boarding house where he was drinking.
He pleaded with the undertaker to delay
removing the body before he had a chance
to address it. So insistent was he
that he was granted his request and spent the night
reading poems over a dead man's body,
expecting a resurrection to rival Lazarus.
All night long he chanted his best work
and finally descended, haggard and dispirited.
It is the power of language that it doesn't
need to tell you how the story ends: it is
the crispness of pine, after the air of summer.

On a Line from CK

Those days of the snow, of wincing out
the bright window as if not only distance
but time itself might appear, and not its effects.
For that moment only, I keep the days
in their own recess in memory's theater.
And the processional flow of the Hudson
when you were not there. And yet
I hugged sorrow as if it were joy.
It was sorrow. The world was tipping
like a boy I pulled from the balcony rail
once in Dublin, so drunk he was delirious
and never felt the hands that yanked him
back into life. For that moment only,
he was free. And I was pulled back
though I knew the hands that took me,
the arms when I came to rest, the face
near mine, the sweet, improbable smell.
Those days when I only waited for time
to mill its grain through me, never seeing
how that same time hastened to rescue me.
Until one night, at the peak of love
she bit my face hard and drew blood
and then fell back like Eurydice
into the dark pillows without a cry,
before and after rushing to the border
for that moment only, separating us.

Helmets

Then there was Pavarotti singing,
"*Donna non vidi mai*" above the random talk
of bookish patrons. Like always,
I waited, a grown man, for the tears;
strangely they didn't come.
I am already on the other side,
I thought, that I can get the sign
and let it pass. Here, where
the paintings are so dark no light
can show what they depict, it was like
being wedged between Caravaggios,
except that there was no source of light.
Here I met the great poet frequently,
when I was the junior great poet,
but that was years ago.
We had espressos and ransacked the world
for the seeds of poems so as not
to be cut off like an unfinished sentence.
He died in his sleep, I am told.
Again with the Pavarotti, and still
no tears, still no signal and no light
on the field of the paintings.
But you can make out a pewter
helmet on one, and then another:

one tilted, one as if looking sideways.
Why were we not expecting this?
What kind of soldiers are we?

Infidel

One day I will find myself tired
of the unique and stylish dispatches,
the small news that hides the big:
a moment that passed in silence
by a brick wall, while in another place
a small moan, muffled by his body.
One day, the words will run out.
I will open the book, and they will
have left only the merest intimation
that they once stood like defenders
of the throne, the T's stiff as halberds,
the shield-like C, and the others.
One day there will be no reason to know
I held you up, as I had been taught,
by poets who thrived on impossible tasks
and while they were alive, boasted
to each other, competing for the most
outlandish claim, the one not to be
undone, the truth so steady that time
itself must withdraw, bowing.
But mostly it will be odd and doubtless
boring to have been of service so long,
contradicting the real and the obvious
like political advisers in a dictatorship,
like Mugabe reciting the little he knows
of T. S. Eliot and then the staffers applaud.

Miss Tilley

My friends went in fear of Miss Tilley,
as did I. And yet we were enjoined
by our young mothers and fathers
to take Latin, since it was "the key
to English" and all that lay beyond.
That steely partridge made cold calls
while we sat, wishing ourselves smaller
and smaller still, finally invisible,
parsing Caesar. "*Gallia est omnis divisa
in partes tres,*" droned the dictator.
"You can only parse verbs," she admonished,
"You can't parse a noun, much less
a sentence." Flushed out for humiliation,
one by one, we took pride in survival.
The T.W.I.U. had called out a strike,
and I followed my father as he paced,
placard in fist, past the smudge pots
lighting the factory's locked doors.
My mother stockpiled canned goods,
then filled boxes for the union hall.
The oily fires burned for days,
the black smoke sagging in air.
There was Belgium and Aquitaine.
And the third? That I forget: so what?
Men willingly believe what they wish,

as Caesar remarked later.
Miss Tilly died unmarried. I used
to pass her house, which seemed
as shut as a tucked-away jewel casket.
Who knows what might have been
stored there, as if put by, as if
looking out, so late, so long ago,
a great deal was on her mind?

Out of the Past

It would be in the evening
in front of the TV, you would
put your leg over mine.
And we would sit like that
with Anderson Cooper,
watching the world going
to hell, watching *The West Wing*.
The table before us held fruit
and nuts, cheese and olives.
A scene from a banal marriage,
perhaps, but that was
the magic of it: a whole year
in that house, with the suspicious
neighbors next door. Then *Laura*
and *Out of the Past,* and I would
take your foot and rub it.
Then the other, pressing the arch
carefully, working the muscular
tightness, the tough heel, ball,
and toes, bones and ligaments.
It had a rhythm like a song
wrapped around a refrain
in which all you ever meant
and all you desire are folded in
an artless verse. It was hand's

version of love songs composed
in a chamber by someone
remembering love, not living
in its company. But then, they
were feet being made ready.
When I held them they pointed
toward heaven. When I put them
down, they pointed away.

Dream Baby

A covey of burqas goes by the laundry,
travel agent, and bar; babies roll along,
concealed in layers in strollers.
Men clustered, the conversation,
whether sports or politics, serious.
Russians stare at the Greeks
and the Greeks stare back at the Russians,
no suspicion, no swapping talk, either.
It's the ultimate, isn't it?
How in this weather, the individual
man shears off from the collective,
and the collective must only wait
a short length to find him again,
that individual now coming up the block,
flushed, cap askew. Where was he?
Someplace where the shadow hesitated,
no doubt. Immigrants in eddies,
a buttery sunlight in a world of sorrow.
I have often thought I should turn from the world
to live in the poem, like the man in the tree
who pulls the ladder up after him,
as if to wed the anonymous and the personal
among the leaves, the clattering branches,
there in the wild perfection of the tree.
Or to stand suddenly among set pieces

and floor exercises, imagining how it will be
not to move, a squirrel on the forest floor
betraying presence with an uncontrollable flick,
while the spirit he remembers moves
by his immobile face in the form of a breeze.
Of my bona fides let it be said,
it was only the life I wouldn't possess,
or that wouldn't own me, that was
my text. Now I forage for the key:
the square or the round? I forget.
Like an acorn or a booster falling away,
even the Beloved, who in my dreams
made care a spotted fruit and death
a feather: reduced to a period.
A man raps inaudibly on the door.
The light in the upstairs window
is small, but it covers everything.

Skunk

I could work it this way and that
but the handle had its own idea.
I closed the door before my face anyway.
It was full of its own flaked bearing
like one leg crossed over the other.
My small porch: Chekhovian, descending
nowhere, railed around and lifted up
by old, grainy posts, which pointed
to the sky ruffling the evening
after rain. A wasp hovered nearby,
then inserted its flickering pitch
into a hole in the drainpipe where
looped wires hooked up. I was surrounded
by the summer evening heft and heard
the last birds that could be made out
crossing the sky in the direction of the mountain.
One cloud in a slow-moving mass held
that it was best to be rounded, salmon-
edged toward the west, teal on the obverse.
Then it dulled in a slow-motion,
almost imperceptible wobble, merging
with the night like the smell of skunk.
Nobody was saying why this should be
or why the willow stood still by the river.

Flame

You wake up one day
and there are people's umbrellas
maneuvering between cars.
And blocked sidewalks.
Someone speaks loudly as if giving
orders in a language you can't
make out. His voice goes by
in the Doppler Effect.
Rain mutes color: blue,
red always. Flame is
rendered as neon, for instance,
like that sign that lights up
the old Pearl Paint building,
now boarded and locked,
and yet someone pays
continually for service.

The one you love turns
as plums do, left too long
in the same place.
The change feels instantaneous
but is not. My friend tells
of shoving her dead father
back into the grave in a recurrent dream.
He just kept reemerging, and she knew

forgiveness could not have meaning
until he had been dead long enough
to be actually hopeless.
Then resurrection is a thing,
if you push the bodies back.
It's raining after all. It wouldn't do
to pretend miracles on so
fresh a closing.

As If

It's said that the sentence, "I am alone"
is a contradiction, since utterance
all by itself implies a recipient
and hence the presence of another, intended
or real. Ironically, it's such rationalizing
that leads to loneliness in the first place
for aloneness is unremarkable, if
not unremarked. I watched a yellow,
violin-shaped patch of sunlight today
on the wall and waited to see if slow time
would allow me to observe light's creep.
Then a stratus cloud over my shoulder,
backed up by the upstate winter sky,
abruptly cancelled the test with the finality
of Michelangelo, who is said to have
critiqued a beseeching pupil's sculpture
by slamming it into a wall.
My new study was bare, except for a desk,
unpainted, and three unmatched chairs.
There were plenty of windows,
as if to say to the loneliness: come,
let the day itself, so full of time, absorb you,
exchanging *seem* for *seen*, *lonely* for *alone*,
with no loose ends, no toxic byproduct.
But the *Inferno* tells a different story,

how in the harrowing the granite split
and the mine was suddenly in danger
of catastrophic collapse, a menacing silt
streaming from the cracks and seams,
not to mention the demons with iron gaffs,
charcoal monkeys and their obscenities.
It would have been the destruction of hell.
The real battle was with the poet's words,
which were the weapons of choice,
hived in clichés, stuttering with imprecision,
until having secured the puzzled hostages,
the unspoken hero led them back through
the very cracks and still-smoking holes
that were the result of the intrusion,
the red-hot inches and dark discriminations.
Even as a rumor, it was what it was,
keeping just one step ahead of the devil,
as my grandmother used to say,
bending the note until it was almost a question,
before turning back to the sink.

Stay

When we had walked the length of Warren Street,
my daughter asked me, in the sweetly
patronizing way of clever girls, how old
Maurice Williams had been when he
and The Zodiacs recorded the classic
two-minute position-paper on longing:
"Stay," complete with its own wish-
fulfillment charm: "Say that you will."
I said he must have been in his twenties,
the decade that aligns artifice
with sincerity, after which it's a chore
to sustain any falsetto lament.
At the same time, I pointed out, he was
all over YouTube warbling his hit,
Bogarting the mic like every one-hit wonder,
through the non-sequitur decades,
to bobbing Bandstand teens, variety shows,
and of course, soul revivals, and he
could be seen there at diverse ages,
the question of high notes notwithstanding.
O Stay! Thou art so fair, cried Faust to Helen,
in translation. We were about to board
a train that follows the river into the city,
where the announcement would take place,
the day finally at hand. The Hudson,

frozen in misty, extruded chunks,
was like an executive takedown of the gentle
ticking of the ice flow in Lowell's poem,
whose puzzle-piece blanks seemed
to bear some mystery beneath, some image,
instead of what they really were—
pate-gray on either side, with no figure
to reassemble, either in the mind of God
or in the passage—parade, really—
by the sense-making city. In other words,
it was hard, dazzlingly crisp, dead-
brilliant with the hush of the north.
Houses balanced on ledges and banks,
later along the flaky Palisades like redoubts
of some cold war unrecorded, but not therefore
unexperienced. People died out there
as the river, so the hymn tells us, bore them,
although it seemed a solid floor too. I
thought how the long street down to the river
seemed with their shops and houses
to bear our recent impression, the seal
of a common life, now hooked into its drift,
content to board. For a moment I thought back
to the summer before, when we had strolled
down it, hand in hand, determined to resist
and be, momentarily, so far from the water.

Pigeons

I was waiting for the pigeons to come,
one who has a place picked out
on the sill above the street vendors
and a partner who sometimes
has a place, sometimes not. They hunch
like footballs in an equipment room.
I would sum up their relationship this way:
if B follows A, then B is its elegy.
In this picture, pigeon B is the lesser,
the suitor, the elegist, although
to the casual observer they look identical—
of an unexceptional gray, but
dappled like the muted sunlight
in Gerard Manley Hopkins.
Code for the inscrutable: those
old battles, still undecided, still
being waged in unlikely places.
The street is crowded and loud,
people wearing hats and scarves.
Some old guy in Washington Square
feeds the pigeons, tossing crumbs
overhead and around his feet.
You can imagine the commotion.
The cell phones close in on a man
covered in birds. Ridiculous. And yet,

where will you be when I am covered,
spreading my arms until I am transformed
and obscured in near useless feathers?

The Complaint

The old poets used to complain about their
significant others. It was a kind of requirement.
They were cruel or remote, or cruel *and* remote.
Also cold, of course, and disinterested.
The categories are unacceptable, now that
centuries of repetition and variation have left
them devoid of descriptive force. Not only that,
but the setup, from an analytical standpoint,
is quite unsatisfactory: objectification, the gaze
and all that. We worked hard to hone
these skills into useful shape, instruments
to look beyond the pretenses and conventions.
They reduce sentiments to what they really are
and so uncover the secret springs and motives
where once there seemed to be a simple, universal cry
that said, I don't think X loves me, and I am
in pain! To which already we could go
in a hundred directions, each tailor-made
to register the unique soul that's going to die.
Questions rise like curling steam, that ask
why did he not escape the common fate, why
did his singularity not move his love to pity?
Why, once the collapse had begun, did it seem
to be unstoppable, joined to the arrow of time,
like necessity, which knows no angel mighty

enough to come down on the side of the poets,
those complaining creatures, who rather
look around, and seeing nothing, begin
in tears their uniform lament. Because it was
nothing itself: no lover, no message, no pity,
a position endorsed by God himself for the next
to order up the light, those monomaniacs dying
to illuminate a vastness into which they
and their loves were destined. God could have said,
it's not so good, but He didn't: He said quite
the opposite. Who are the young poets to jump in
and complain again? The point is, a world spun
out of that nothing, and here we are lined up,
goodness on one side, grievances on the other.

The Red Dot

After we embraced at the crosswalk
in the coarse fidelity of separation
our chests together one brief last time

in the rain, in the bluster, the puddles,
the honking taxis, the herds of umbrellas,
then my family rose from their silos

and crossed the sky to find me.
My mother and father like a flying
boxcar, my father with his trumpet,

then my brother with the hole
in his temple untouched, soaring
up the east coast, practically

stratospheric, like a hawk in autumn,
whose vision increases with distance,
looking to find me, past the forests

of Pennsylvania, past the Pine Barrens,
finally turning east before Paterson,
down through swirling pipes of rain,

the dark copper clouds, the towers
rising from the river, the shining rooftops,
my mother and father swerving out,

then turning in from the sea, looking
to land, looking for their other son,
the one who had summoned them

and my brother whose eternal muteness
would someday become speech,
and that pass for eloquence, as

Nietzsche himself reassured us. I came
home and sat by the computer screen
checking, as I had always done,

for the ruby dot announcing a message,
light that burns a hole in everything,
a change of heart as if the heart were

no longer hurtling into the rain, no longer
losing, anxiously whispering, *change me!*
Instead I heard them overhead.

I looked up and we smiled at each other.
I was being airlifted by beloved
spirits called to the old vastness

from the sleep of their cylinders,
who bore my name, who still believed,
sleepy as they were, that they knew me.

Up we went and I saw Canal shrink
into a line, the line into a spinning
propeller, so I looked straight up, my family

pulling me up in the updraft, through
the plunging temperatures, until it was
full black, and yet there were stars.

Here they peeled off and faded,
leaving me; they were just clouds
themselves now, morphing and turning.

Because I was vexed, I pretended
it was them. Because there was no
red dot, only black city rain,

I found myself floating, knowing
how Pluto would rise from his throne
pointing earthward, not heavenward,

though I was exalted in my wedding suit
waiting to have my ears rubbed,
which was the special sign for love

for no one could mistake thinking
that's what it's like. Not even
the sweet dead in their cerements.

Not even a stranger.

The Porch

The upper porch is rickety and could come loose
at any time. A black mud dauber
lands on a square of sunlight, rotates
for a moment on a two-by-four, then is gone.
Nervous sleep and day demanding: Diesels
hum between some trees and the hot sky,
which has dismissed any chatter of clouds.
An old gray cat, like the past, drags its long tail
through the gravel. Shadows move across the siding
like Plato's cave where he sits, perched. Without being
there, he knows what the river is doing:
it's the same thing that marks the appearance
of the creatures: groundhog, skunk, a nearly invisible fawn
he spotted between the woods and the road
when he came down the mountain, seeds wandering, falling
like cotton from the tall trees. They were en route
happy enough to be blind in the landing, just as the trees
shook them off indifferently. He could draw
the lesson, but in his singularity, does not.
Better to end on the images, as the poet said, let them form
from the void, take whatever shape is theirs
and like the old masters of figure and ground, go from that.

The King of Thebes

There were the barefoot girls in see-through dresses,
and she had been one of them. She pauses to let that
sink in. Just then a house wren flies up to the window,
looks in curiously and darts out of the frame.
He knew them too, so many summers back, so many
towns-with-a-square ago. His were different beaches,
some with bunkers that spoke of an even older time,
all with the rippling sea grass, as if people leaned
against a cordon, waving to their favorite movie stars
who stepped from limousines, faultless in tuxedos
and furs, and made their way to the premiere.
She speaks in a low, conclusive voice across the table,
opens a fresh pack of cigarettes and selects one
from the back row of the pack, like a magician
choosing a helper from the back of the nightclub.
There are no more birds now, and the window frames
her head, the new hair not as glamorous as the old.
Then there is the whisky, which has been sitting on the floor
by her chair, named after a man, himself silhouetted
on the label. She speaks of the first husband, now dead,
how he had squirreled away boxes of porn, even
as he descended into Hades with his memory wronged
by the ghouls sent to pick through his remains.
Pity rises in his mind, though he knows it doesn't belong there.
She pushes the cigarette pack in his direction,

but he only remembers, for a moment, his father hunched
and terminal, and then all those other men
who fought so bravely when the war crashed ashore.
They are small figures now, punctuation marks that guide
the mind across its terrain. He knows the girls
on her beach; they too wish to be accorded a name,
but he can't come up with any. He may have slept with a few
once, but birdsong leaves everything winsome and vague.
She means to say there is greatness abounding
in small amounts, blowing smoke that the screen catches
and directs outside. His pity is abstract to her,
like a ceremony where presence is a placeholder, when men
in suits stand silently by women in dark gowns,
having discharged the obligations of the outside
to the inner force that drives the bridegroom to unite
with the sailor. But she is a friend to such sacrifices,
and she deserves the bottle at her foot, the whisky
she sips from a cup, as though it were the King of Thebes
who offered up a toast, lest the war be forgotten,
lest it be turned over to the bird, still audible
above the angry traffic, the horns, and the jackhammer.

Some Sweet Day

Chipmunks on the rocks, and earlier,
deer. Sun comes through the leaves,
climbs, and the leaves show their veins,
then dim to their default.
The yard slopes down to a stream,
and a woman stands on the porch.
She turns her head and sings,
but there is no song, only
light in swells, as if light were
a figured music. Soon, neither
the soughing in the layers,
nor the trifling arpeggios,
the "long-winded peeps"
of unseen birds will remain, only tires
from the nearby highway, rolling
and approaching, then rounding,
and someone gunning the engine
of a motorcycle. One is caught
between weariness and surmise,
praising time and looking
at the woods like a frame maker
working around a portrait, first
carving, then nailing and gluing,
as if unaware of the subject,
though, of course, awareness is there.

Why else would the woman
disappear indoors, at seed-fall,
her song not a song, her residue
surrendered to the rocks
scattered about the stream
like histories glowing in sunlight,
while the porch, the prow of a ship
named "Some Sweet Day"
by its secret, unpolished captain,
rises and falls in the swells?

A Breakfast

Daddy is fixing breakfast this morning:
country ham, fried eggs, grits and red-eye.
He calls it "breakfast of champions."
My mother is pinning the wash to the line.
I can see her through the window, bending
to the basket, standing up, an assembly line.
I'm embarrassed at the row of underwear,
but why? The neighbors have their lines.
An earwig pops out and wiggles across the sill.
Then my brother emerges, stands sullen
in the doorway, before sitting at his place.
Not much to say, and yet so much unsaid,
so much we bring to the table, its thin
white tablecloth that touches our knees
as we sit. Before long, we will all be
heading out, under the crop of our masters.
But not this morning: time has no business here.
What the mockingbird can't see, as it
perches flickering in the bush, neither
will it sing, as the day brightens.
Neither will I sink to interpretation,
who sing, and forfeit the dead.

The Earwig

The way chance spaced the trees
gives the eye a runway to the black point
just before the turnpike, itself
invisible, until the leaves burn
and finish. If I had a soul—
and who's to say I can't sing
in these terms?—that's where
I would find it, that dark spot
looking back at me, if, that is,
it could look back through
the young trees to the old
and the dead still rising on the bank
of the brook, as if they too had
a purpose and stood as tall
as the sky allowed. But I am here,
where an earwig, paused on the slate,
stirs and begins making its way
across the flecked, moving surface,
as if in dance, but there is no dance,
just yes and no in sequential volley,
rendered by leaf-shade and sunlight,
just as Hopkins described it
a hundred and fifty years ago,
only minus belief, just crawling,
nothing simpler, on its way to the soil.

Not the Mighty but the Weak

It was in a library, or, what passed for a library
in an old house on the leeward side of a hill.
He could not hear the ocean, but it was there,
over the other hills, and sent clouds scudding
far inland. The leaves, furious, were falling.
He thought to blow them over the edge
so as to build the hill. There had been a stone
wall that went down to the stream, but it had
collapsed under some regime no one remembers.
There was Emerson, of course, and Pierce
and certain other madmen whose souls
reverberated in the silence of the books:
buckram and board, jaundiced paper, glue and thread.
He knew the condition and pitch of each soul,
but not of his own, for his life had spread,
extending first forward, then through memory.
But now it had mysteriously circled back upon itself.
Death was spreading through him now
because death was jealous of the intricate tracery
his life had arrogated to itself. But death's decline?
Death's *own* dying? That was the thing.
The comity of the dead, for whom
he had scant breath. Yet he was custodian.
Then Emerson said, "Do not mistake the thunder
for the verse. The incomprehensible poem

is the truest." He also said other things,
or so the custodian thought, but mostly
it was the unremitting fury of the leaves,
the yawing of the shelves where he paced,
and sheets of dust. All the same, the house
stood, and the clouds crossed over in ranks,
their shadows through the window
passing over the stacks whose spines
darkened momentarily. The stream felt
them too, and took them briefly in
before taking them altogether, as if
completion was a subject fit for a library
whose freshest word murmured anxiously,
on and on, from an impossible distance.

Acknowledgments

My gratitude to The National Endowment for the Arts for a Fellowship in Literature, The Pushcart Foundation and The Jentel Foundation for a residency. I also wish to thank the editors of the following, where many of these poems first appeared:

The Galway Review, The Gladstone Readings Anthology, The Greensboro Review, Inertia Magazine, Main Street Rag, A New Ulster, Nine Mile, One, Poetry Northwest

Rigsbee is the author *The Pilot House* (winner of the 2009 Black River Chapbook Competition), *School of the Americas*, and *Not Alone in My Dancing: Essays and Reviews*, all from Black Lawrence Press. His translation of Dante's *Paradiso* will be published by Salmon Poetry in 2018. He has been recipient of two creative writing fellowships from the National Endowment for the Arts, as well as a NEH summer fellowship to the American Academy in Rome. His other awards include a Pushcart Prize, The Fine Arts Work Center in Provincetown fellowship, The Virginia Commission on the Arts literary fellowship, The Djerassi Foundation and Jentel Foundation residencies, and an Award from the Academy of American Poets. He is a contributing editor to *The Cortland Review*.